I0487014

"Two feet walk into a bar..."

"Hear what others don't,

to get what others won't."

Author: *A. J. Gallagher*

Dedicated to:

This book is dedicated to my wife whom

I love dearly; also to my son, Joseph and

my God whom I serve. Also, this book

could not have been written without my

Father who taught it – or my Mother

who has always loved and inspired me.

Table of Contents:

Prologue

I was born in Cleveland Ohio and I am the baby of 10 children; *I still get a kick out of telling people that.* Life had many advantages and disadvantages; and although hand me downs were plentiful, gifts like wisdom and/or praise were tough to come by from the brothers and sisters. We definitely loved each other – but, being of Irish *(and just a tiny touch of Pennsylvania Dutch – sorry Mom)* descent, we were very good at showing

love 'with a little force'. I guess you
would call that - tough-love.

We were raised by a career Mother; who
tried daily to feed and clothe us well and
teach us right from wrong. Our Father,
Farrell Gallagher, worked hard all his
life. He held as many as three jobs at
once, just to make sure that the ends
met. Truly, as a large and not exactly
rich family, we wanted for nothing.
Shoes, clothes, food, shelter and an
excellent work ethic; are all gifts that we
received from both of our parents.

In Cleveland, there is a half-way house for people suffering from drug and alcohol addictions called *Stella Maris*, which would not exist were it not for my Father.

The unfortunate part of this story is a thing called Diabetes. At around fifty years old, it started (not-so slowly) taking my Dad apart. So, in a relatively short time, my Father ended having bad feet, a massive stroke and high blood pressure, and then he lost his eyesight to Glaucoma.

This disease processes started just after we moved from Cleveland, Ohio to the Fort Lauderdale area in Florida. As you can imagine, this changed our financial situation dramatically. In just over a years' time, we went from not really wanting for anything to living in low-income housing and living on food stamps. For many years we (Mom, Dad, two sisters and two brothers) lived in that 3 bedroom low-income apartment. I know this had to be difficult on both parents – but sickness became much more of a priority for them than money and work. Dad had gone downhill very

quickly.

Although it was an extremely difficult

time for him; as well as the rest of the

family – we still had much that we could

learn from our Father. From what I

gather about my Father, he had always

been good at assessing people and

personality types. He was definitely one

of those staunch men who; if he did not

like you – you stayed not liked.

Of all the things he lost when his

eyesight went – his ability to read

people was not one of them – it was just altered. Simply by listening, he could not only tell who was entering the room, he could also tell their mood.

As a teenager, I never put much stock into this skill – until I began working semi-serious jobs.

Then I realized something; it does not matter where you work. Whether you are working at a grocery store, as I did when my ears were opened, or an office setting, or in a hospital (where I am now). There is something we can all

learn from this former 'seeing' man.

What you'll understand is that if you

can raise your awareness to knowing

who is near you and what their mood is

– you can prepare yourself for just about

any situation.

The How's and Why's

of What I've Learned

A teenager of 13 years walks in to his family's apartment. He walks through the kitchen (across a vinyl floor) and turns left to pass through the dining room. As soon as he turns; an impressive figure (Dad was a big man) who is sitting on his favorite recliner, says; "Hi Tony, how was your day?" From any other person, this might be expected – but this was different...the man was blind.

After a few times like this, I was getting

just a little freaked out by it. Of course,

to him, it was routine. No matter the

time of day, or day of the week – he

seemed to always know who was

entering the house.

Finally, I had to know. So I asked him

how he could always tell who was

entering the house. His explanation fell

upon dead ears (that of a teenager),

until later in life when his answer came

back to me with amazing revelation.

Here was his answer, as best as I can

remember:

"Everybody's walk has a personality.

When you come in, I can tell that it's you

because there is a skip in your step.

One of your sister's drags her left foot

just a little. As long as I am listening, I

can always tell who is at the door. If I

am listening closely enough, I can even

tell what mood you are in by the way

your walk changes."

It was not until I became the supervisor of a mobile ultrasound company that I began to understand and 'hone' this skill.

There were two 'bosses'; a President and a Vice President, one was a friend to the staff, the other was the guy who was; for lack of a better term - the taskmaster. Each had a distinct walk: The friend to the staff (and Vice President), was a former ultrasound tech, he understood the staff and they were relaxed around him. He had a casual stride with a slight shuffle. He was definitely a 'Shuffler'. If you knew he was coming, you could relax and when he got there you could enjoy your conversation. He understood that if there was nothing to do at the present time – you did just that, nothing. You felt comfortable around him and when he was approaching, you did not need to change anything.

The other (The President of the company) was stiff and serious. He was the money cruncher. When he came around, you had better look busy. His

walk was purposeful, distinct and loud.

He wanted to make sure that his

presence was known. He was definitely

a 'Stalwart'. If he was coming by your

office or desk; you had better be busy.

Or, at least look like it.

This was the point where I realized that

knowledge of who was nearby could

come in very handy. So I began my own

little study of foot sounds and

personalities.

Basically, once I got beyond the selfish minded teenage and early 20's; I realized that my Father had taken a disability and changed it into a skill that I could use in my everyday life.

Over the last 15 years, this book has written itself. I have jotted down notes on what I have heard and what I have learned. The most important thing that you will learn within this book is that you must LISTEN. Listening may be a lost art, but at least it is an art that almost anyone can learn.

Just a final note on this book...If you are

a 'professional' I want you to realize the

following. This is not a book that a

learned professor worked for years on a

thesis to present. It is not a study in

personality types: Although, that is

included in this book. It is a practical

guide on listening to your surroundings

and knowing what can be learned from

them.

The Layout of the Book

Simply put, each of the following three
chapters will be laid out in a similar
fashion. There are three sections:

Sound Description:

This is a brief explanation of how a
particular type of person walks and
what you should listen for.

Traits:

You will learn the traits or personalities
of the person who walks with those
sounds.

Sound Description Changes:

How the sound of their walk changes
when their mood is different.

Thought Breaks:

I am a fan of writing notes in a book
that has some meaning to me. So often
when reading a book like this; you may
have a response to what is written. This
can happen in the form of ideas,
responses to statements or even notes
about people who fit into a particular
category. When this happens, if you
have a mind like my own – these

thoughts may soon leave you if not written. This thought break page allows you to jot your ideas for later perusal.

Another benefit for the Thought Break is...It may be helpful to take a note or two about your own workspace. As you listen to each person walk by, you will be able to figure out what walk type a person has and where they would get placed into this book.

Finally, the last chapter will give you some practical advice how to use this new skill to your advantage. How much we pay attention to our surroundings

will determine what you can gain – or

lose.

Let's be frank – any new skill that you

learn can only help your career.

The art of listening has always been

extremely powerful – it just got even

more so.

The Personality of a Walk

Remember, all you have to do is…listen.

Or as someone wiser than I said,

"He who has ears to hear; let him hear."

The Holy Bible, Matthew 4:9

A brief internet search for Personality

Tests brought up 3,320,000 results in

0.10 seconds. I looked at the first 30

results and they were all seemingly

legitimate web sites with personality
tests. So why should I bother
presenting another one?

I shouldn't...Truth be told, this is far
less a personality profiler than it is an
office and career help guide. In the little
bit of time it takes to read this book –
you will greatly increase your ability to
present yourself properly to whoever
approaches your desk. I have no doubt
that this book is a good investment in
you.

People and people groups have been

classified in personality profiles by

colors, letters, a series of fancy terms

that no one uses - and even whether or

not they have phlegm. After reading

this book, you will be able to classify

them by their walk –and more

importantly, you will be able to tell who

is coming, what kind of person they are

and what mood they are in.

Every step, every pace is about as

individual as a thumbprint. Line up

three different people and have them

walk by your door.   *Of course, if you*

have a door – keep it open so you can

actually hear them coming. Then close

your eyes and listen. You'll discover a

whole new world of understanding; they

will all have different sounds; I call

these *Sound Distinctions.* Now take a

moment and match the Sound

Distinction to those individuals. Then

commit that to memory and you'll

always know when those people are

approaching your desk.

As a child, I used to love watching

Westerns – I was a big John Wayne fan.

All those movies about cowboys and

Indians, good guys vs. bad guys, made

for wonderful boyhood movies. I

remember the specialists of that time –

they were called trackers and they could

track anybody anywhere. The really

good ones could not only tell you which

way someone went, but also who, if

anybody was following you.

They would get down off their horse, get

on their hands and knees and put their

ear to the ground. Then they would look up and say something like, "there are 4 riders after us, three on horseback and one on a horse drawn carriage. Their moving slowly because it sounds like one of the horses is coming up lame." Ok, I embellished n the "lame" part – but you get my drift.

I remember thinking how amazing those men were – of course at that time, I didn't realize that it was just a movie.

Those trackers are who we need to be like in our everyday life. Aside from listening to volume and whether or not you hear the heel and toe sounds; also listen for the personalities of their feet. Remember, my Father knew me because I had a skip in my walk and knew my sister because she tended to drag one foot. You will need to memorize and know these Sound Distinctions. Which like everything else; comes easily with repetition.

CAUSALITY

In the second movie of The Matrix series, The Matrix Reloaded, there is a great scene when Morpheus, Neo and Trinity go visit the Frenchman (an information gatherer). He goes on this little speech about Causality. Causality is the set of events or forces that presumably brought all of them to that point in time.

Here is what the Frenchman said about it: "You see there is only one constant. One universal. It is the only real truth.

Causality. Action, reaction. Cause and effect..."

"...What is the reason? Soon the why and the reason are gone and all that matters is the feeling. This is the nature of the universe. We struggle against it, we fight to deny it but it is of course a lie. Beneath our poised appearance we are completely out of control."

I am using the word causality to explain what causes a person to walk like they do. We really have no control over it; we do not put thought behind it. As the man said; 'soon the why and reason are gone and all that matters is

the 'Footsounds'. Just as everything in your
past and present makes us who we are. These
same life events also change your walk.

Are you musically minded? Then you truly do
'walk to a different beat' and your
'footsounds' will display that.

Happy-go-lucky people will general walk with
a quicker pace and will have some sort of skip
to their walk – fortunately for those who listen,
this skip is repetitious and recognizable.

A sad or generally melancholy person
will tend to drag their feet. Again,

whatever in their life is causing their

mood – it affects their walk.

Let me address medical issues briefly

and how they affect a persons walk –

and I will ignore the obvious. The

obvious being foot, leg and hip problems.

Aside from those, a shoulder problem

can cause someone to walk heavier on

the opposing foot. They are trying to

compensate for pain – giving you easy

recognition of who is approaching your

desk or work area. A person with lung

and breathing trouble generally has

very heavy feet and will with shuffle or

drop their feet heavily with each step.

"Work hint... do you work in retail?

How great of an asset would you be if

you could assess a customer as they

approached and know if they are going

to need physical assistance – even before

you speak to them? Your career path

could soar, simply by maximizing your

customer service."

The next few chapters will cover the types of walks you will encounter and the general type of personalities that have that particular walk. As you read, you may notice that when a Butterfly gets upset, that persons' walk may sound like a Stalwart. This is where recognizing a person's natural walk comes in handy. The skip in the step or the drag of one foot will never leave them. It stays no matter what their mood.

Prepare to be prepared.

The STALWART

Webster's dictionary defines stalwart as firm, steadfast, or uncompromising. This is the type of individual whose footsteps that I am about to describe.

Sound Description:

Volume: Generally loud – this personality expects to be heard and listened to.

Distinction: Both heel and toe sounds can be distinctly heard.

Personality type:

This is generally a strong/confident individual. They tend to be leaders in there arena – whether by title or simply because of who they are.

The sounds of their feet represent a person of purpose; everything to them has a purpose and a goal and their walk is no different. They perform every act (including walking) as if what they do is ultimately important.

The Stalwart is usually a manager or supervisor. They border on

perfectionism. Lines are their friend
and they will expect people to follow
them.

Even if he or she is not in a manager
position, people will view him as a
leader in whatever arena they are in.

The Stalwart will make for solid friends
and employees; but expect them to fix
things (even in relationships) that they
deem to be wrong or fixable.

How the Sound Distinction Changes

For the Stalwart – the main change is in

pace.

Faster/Lighter sound: This means that

they are anxious – but a good anxious.

The term "light on their feet" would fit

this mood. If a Stalwart is approaching

with this sound change, expect good

news of some kind. At least, expect

them to be in a good mood.

Slower/Louder: This person has heavy

feet; but not because of physical weight.

If this sound change occurs – clear your

desk and brace yourself. Some sort of
bad news is coming.

I worked with a Radiology Director at a
certain Medical Center who was a
Stalwart. She was a highly aggressive,
go-getter of an individual; very nice, yet
very professional. She had worked her
way up by being aggressive and
assertive. She was always taking
classes and updating her knowledge of
her field. She had done everything to
deserve that position and knew that she
was not done. Her attire was always

perfect and her footsounds definitely made a statement.

When things were going well, her heel and toe sounds were almost musical. The way they clicked in perfect rhythm let everyone know that her world was in perfect order. Loud, crisp...anyone who listened knew when she was in the area and that things were going well.

However, when things weren't right...you knew (or at least I did). If she was in a bad mood, her footsounds got louder; she pounded those feet. Also, her heels had a double-click sound to them; I can guess that this was due to the type of shoe she wore. When I heard this sound coming, I knew that it was best to leave the area – rather than face the brunt of whatever had set her off that day.

It is by listening that I was best able to serve her as an employee and be prepared for where the next conversation might take me.

<u>Thought Breaks</u>

Chapter 5

The SHUFFLER

Named for the sound their feet make; generally a stand up, even tempered individual.

Sound Description:

Volume: Soft to Mildly loud.

Distinction: Generally, there is no distinct heel or toe sound; just a prolonged noise – a shuffle.

Personality type:

This is generally an even tempered individual. They have the ability to be a leader, but generally don't take those reigns. They prefer to be part of the team, a solid worker-bee.

They will get through their work day with little or no trouble. For a manager, they are low maintenance personnel. Rarely are they distracted from their task.

The Shuffler is a self-paced worker; some people may consider them lazy or slow as far as production is concerned.

But just like we all learned in the race

against the turtle and the hare – don't

count them out. Whether it's personal

or business, they can always be counted

on to complete their task.

These are solid individuals who will

make for stable friends and employees.

How the Sound Distinction Changes

For the Shuffler – due to their

personality, there is minimal change in

their walk. If this person is approaching, you can still tell who. But it can be difficult to tell their mood.

However, when they are anxious, their pace will quicken and their shuffle will get softer (lower in volume). This quickening in pace is generally a good sign and you will enjoy the conversation you are about to have.

Thought Breaks

The BUTTERFLY

The term butterfly was chosen because this person routinely has butterflies in their stomach. They tend to be emotion driven and are easily distracted.

Sound Description:

Volume: Medium volume; definitely a "notice me" volume.

Distinction: Generally, the toe sound only is heard.

Personality type:

This is the person whose home-life routinely invades their work-life (and visa versa). They are generally anxious and in a "harried" state of mind as they tend to feel that things are out of control.

The mainly toe-only sound is generally due to their 'Living life on the edge' personality. But, it's not the extreme (Kick-boxing in the Himalayas) kind of extreme. But rather the life is coming at me too fast kind of life on the edge.

The Butterfly has a lot of friends, but even their friends realize that there are times to just stay back and give them space. They don't handle changes or corrections well and need to be left alone to process things.

As employees: they are dedicated and conscientious workers. But when events happen in their life; whether the events are from work or home – you need to give them the space or time they need to recover. Recovery from life's distractions can take anywhere from a few minutes to a couple of hours. Their

production will definitely drop during

that time – but as a manager, consider

this a minimal loss. Giving them this

'recovery' time goes a long way toward

healing them. Once they recover – they

become even better workers. By

allowing them time to process trials like

this, their loyalty to you will greatly

increase.

Going back to the turtle and the hare

example; this is the hare. The up times

of the Butterfly are so much better

(more productive) and longer lasting
than their down times – you will learn
that the time loss during a down time is
acceptable.

How the Sound Distinction Changes

For the Butterfly – both volume and
sound distinction changes. But, pay
attention to the speed – it is the real
clue giver.

Increased speed: Their pace will
increase whether they are very happy or
concerned. Either way, they just need to
talk. It's time to clear your desk and

your time. You will have to give them

the attention they need so that they can

recover from whatever set them off.

Slower speed: When a Butterfly slows

down, they are extremely troubled.

Whatever the issue may be – it is going

to be major (at lease to them). At this

point, they will even drop a heel;

although the heel sound will not be as

loud as the toe sound.

I worked with a young woman who had

one husband and two children. She was

a steadfast, conscientious worker who

took pride in her work and would stay late to finish whatever tasks she needed to complete; even if she wasn't on the clock.

Her downfall was her family, and her attachments to them. We all love our children dearly and she was no different. However, she felt that she needed to fix her child's problems rather then allow them to learn on their own. Also, it seemed that whenever her child had a problem, it always needed to be fixed while she was at work.

If her child called, with a problem – she

took whatever time was necessary to

talk to them about it – on the clock.

Anyone within earshot would tell you

that she would keep (him) on the phone

until he saw...*and went along with* her

viewpoint.

This employee had a quick pace with a

loud toe sound and a barely audible heel

sound. One day I heard her coming. As

she approached, I noticed two distinct

changes. First, her pace had slowed

considerably. Second, she had switched

from a low heel and a loud toe to a loud

heel and a low toe. Her heels were

hitting so hard, I thought she was

digging them into the floor. I knew she

needed a listening ear before she even

made it to my office – so I had already

minimized the screen on my computer

and made room on my desk so that I

could give her full attention.

This particular day, something major

had occurred in her child's life. I

listened for about fifteen minutes;

offered no advice (as a manager, I only

do this if it is asked), then let her leave.

She spent almost the next hour on the

phone.

As a listening manager; I knew that she

needed to settle things. I also knew that

once she did, her productivity would

increase. In the great scheme of things

– the hourly pay that I lost for her one

hour of non-production time was a good

investment toward keeping a good,

competent and content employee.

"Work hint... if someone comes in your office to talk. STOP what you are doing and listen. It shows that you care; it will also shorten the visit as they will get through what they need to say without repetition as they know you are listening."

Thought Breaks

_____

_____

_____

_____

_____

_____

_____

_____

How to Use This Knowledge

G.I. Joe had a catch phrase: "Knowing is
half the battle."

Every public speaker is taught to know
their audience. No matter who you are
at work, you need to do the same.

The above paragraph may sound cliché,
but I have adopted the idea that I
should always be prepared. You
guessed it – I'm a Stalwart.

When he was young, my Father was an alcoholic. At the time of his death, he had over 30 years of sobriety. Alcoholics Anonymous was the key to helping him and AA had become a major part of our family's lives.

He made it his mission in life was to help others as much as he could; he used to have men come over to our house that he had sponsored or was sponsoring into AA. There would routinely be men in our house that would call him if they

64

needed a drink and he would 'talk them
down'.

Occasionally, my Father would let me
stay in the room when he spoke with
these men; I believe that he was trying
to prevent me from heading down the
path that he had traveled. I can clearly
remember one afternoon (after he had
gone blind) when a man called my
Father because he had the urge to have a
drink. He was told to come over to our
house.

As he entered the house, my Dad told to stay in my room for this one. Although confused, I listened (always better to listen then face Dad's wrath).

Shortly after I left the room, there was a lot of yelling. I could not understand everything that they were saying; and at this point it does not matter. The man left about five minutes after his arrival, obviously angry about something. It ends up that this man had come over drunk and ready for a fight.

Clearly, my Father had some insight that this was going to turn bad. When I asked him about it – he said that he could tell by the way he entered that there was going to be trouble. Curious thing was... the man hadn't spoken two words before Dad sent me away. My guess is; he 'heard' the problem coming by the way the man entered our apartment.

Let's be practical...just by listening, can you really be prepared for whoever and whatever is about to happen in or near your workspace?

The answer is <u>why not</u>? Too many people will tell you that there is a reason that we have two ears and only one mouth. Let's learn how to use these gifts that we have.

Just imagine:

- Always looking busy when your boss arrives. Although this may not be the most upstanding reason for this book – it is very practical. Your ears can be the ultimate "Boss" button.

- If you know that someone is coming to pick up a report and you hear them coming; you can have it in hand and ready for them.

- Always having the right documents on the desk when your manager shows up to pick them up.

- Being mentally prepared when a Butterfly shows up at your desk and sees that you are ready to listen and give them the time they need.

- Having the ability to assess a customer and approach them appropriately.

On a more personal note...imagine:

- Knowing who's coming up your stairs at home.

Or...

- Knowing who is at your front door when you hear them crossing your front or back porch.

A co-worker told me a story of her and her husband vacationing in a cabin. It was late one night and they heard a sound on the porch. They heard footsteps walking across the porch and even heard the handle being turned at the front door. They dressed themselves and quickly looked for some kind of weapon.

Having nothing better, he grabbed a

log from beside the fireplace. By the

time he got to the front door,

whoever it was, had left.

The next morning, two friends of

theirs showed up – they said that

the night before, they had come to

visit. When no one answered the

door, they tried to open it. Once

that failed, they went back home

only to drive up the next day. How

helpful would it be to have known

that what they heard were the

footsounds of their own friends?

Preparing yourself for any situation is

always the key.

Being prepared for almost everyone who

arrives at your desk is a skill that few

have. If you want to get one step ahead

of your competition – learn to listen.

Chapter 8

Epilog

I could easily come up with a dozen
stories of how listening to footsounds
has helped me. Professionally and
personally; knowing who is approaching
you, what their mood is and what kind
of person they are, gives you a great
advantage.

There are too many people judging you
at work. Some want to replace you,
others want to hire you – still others
may want to fire you.

So, it does help to know who is around

you. Listening to who is there will allow

you to know if the people nearby are

there to help or cause harm of some

type. As the military calls it; are they

friend or foe.

Sun Tzu tried to explain it when he said,

"Keep your friends close and your

enemies closer."

No matter where I am; if you're

approaching me – I want to be able to

tell who you are.

All I am striving to impart here is: Be

prepared. Use every weapon that you

have in your arsenal, including that

little used ability...listening.

It has long been said that we have one

mouth and two ears for a reason. Now

we have an even better reason to be still

and listen.

The End